Reflections of Life

Reflections of Life

Rodney D. Edge

Copyright © 2024 Rodney Edge.

All rights reserved. No part of this book may be reproduced, stored, or transmitted by any means—whether auditory, graphic, mechanical, or electronic—without written permission of both publisher and author, except in the case of brief excerpts used in critical articles and reviews. Unauthorized reproduction of any part of this work is illegal and is punishable by law.

ISBN: 979-8-89031-880-0 (sc)
ISBN: 979-8-89031-881-7 (hc)
ISBN: 979-8-89031-882-4 (e)

Because of the dynamic nature of the Internet, any web addresses or links contained in this book may have changed since publication and may no longer be valid. The views expressed in this work are solely those of the author and do not necessarily reflect the views of the publisher, and the publisher hereby disclaims any responsibility for them.

One Galleria Blvd., Suite 1900, Metairie, LA 70001
(504) 702-6708

This is a tribute to all the people whose friendship I cherish, and those whose caring ways I have come to adore. Special thanks to all who have inspired My life in positive ways.

Contents

Love 1
   Three Loves 3
   FRISKY 6
   YOU 8
   CLOSER TO YOU 9
   LOVE IS… 11
   Love Lost 12
   Passion 13
   Friends and Lovers 15
   My Valentine 17

Seduction 19
   SEDUCTION 21
   A KISS 23
   Fantasy 24
   Making Love 26
   Red 28
   I Knew 29
   The Encounter 32

Family 35
   Sis… 37
   Uncles 39

    MOMMA *41*
    Brother *43*
    Cousins *46*

Culture *47*

    WASHINGTON, DC *49*
    CHICAGO *52*
    RELIGION *54*
    Our Land *56*
    My Flava Ain't Your Flava *58*
    NOTES *60*
    GETTING IT ON… *62*
    JAZZ *64*
    THE HOOD *66*
    Black *69*

Tranquility *73*

    Shadow *75*
    Running *77*
    SALVATION *78*
    Sensation *79*
    Joy *80*

Complexity *83*

    Gilded Horse *85*
    JUSTICE *88*
    Keeping Score *90*
    They Were Chosen *92*
    Things People See *96*
    Youth Gone Mad *98*

AFFIRMATIVE ACTION *101*
    Freedom *103*
    What If? *106*

Women 109
    She *111*
    Women *113*
    HER *115*
    Lady *117*
    BEAUTY *119*
    BLACK WOMAN *121*
    THE DRESS *123*
    Beautiful *125*
    PRETTY AND NICE *128*

Oneness 131
    My Wife *133*
    Marriage Pledge *134*
    The One *136*
    Becoming A Man *138*

Nature 141
    Nature *143*
    A ROSE *145*
    WINTER *147*
    FALL *149*
    SEEDLINGS *151*
    Spring *152*
    SUMMER *153*

Love

Three Loves

I met the first as a High School boy…
She was the embodiment of an Olympus God.

Crafted uniquely in every way,
more intriguing than words can say.

With her I graduated to the next level…
Not yet a man, but never the less,
not still a boy.

We walked endlessly on the streets
of our Metropolis.
Never dreamt of beaches…
Our walks home were the tranquil
sedative that relaxed us
after a long school day.

We spoke more than we walked…
Oddly enough, words were never
absent when we talked.

We were best friends…
Best friends to the end.

One day we awakened and
began to drift apart.
Although many decades have past,
she still has my heart.

I met the second during the
maturation of higher learning.
Different from the first,
like the sun and rain…
For the first time my
heart experience pain.

She introduced me to manhood.
In my arms she became a woman.

With my first, the grasp of a hand
and a smile were enough…
My second taught me the
true essence of touch.

My second was probably
the one to be.

She was a polygon trapped
in a prism of light.
Some days I would embrace
her with all my might.

Until the day her touch
felt empty…
Because of something I did
that was so silly.

We still planned a future
that seemed so bright.
I was still not the proposing kind,
I was aloof, without vision and sight.

She took a journey and left
me alone…
If hindsight were my future,
today I would echo a different tone.

My last love I have
yet to meet…
The fairy-tale bride to sweep
me off my feet.

My life companion, the true
love I seek.
I pray I have corrective
vision this time when we meet.

I can't picture what she will be like…
But I relish a happiness seeming unlike…
Anything I ever experienced with
the initial two…
Something borrowed, Something blue.

FRISKY

She was mine, but not in the
be mine frame of mind…
I bought her, but not as
one would buy a woman, or
in the slave property thought process.

We communicated endlessly,
Yet she did not speak English,
nor could she sign or write.

I was her owner, but
she was never in bondage.
She was my child, but
it was impossible for me
to aid in her conception.

She protected me…ever ready
to sacrifice her own life to save mine.

Her kisses brightened my
days, however they were
never indicative of romance.

When I left her alone, each
return was a celebration of joy.
She knew nothing less than
demonstrating boundless affection.

One day she left and my
heart was shattered beyond repair.
My best friend was extinguished
in the flicker of an eye.
Never was I prepared for
her to suddenly die…

My memory of her is
like Titanium.
She can not be replaced, nor
will my thoughts be erased.

She was with me for
only a very short time.
If she were only still
alive, everything would be just fine.

YOU

It's not because of what you
have, but what you do.
It's not because of what you
say, but the person that is you.

It's your smile, your smell,
your touch, your glow…
How do I know?

I know because you put
me before you.
How could I ever give back
anything comparable to the
things you do.

You are the Sun and I
am the Planets…

I am the Stars and you
the Universe.
Never to disperse…
Words spoken so gently.
Because of you, I now see
what it means
to be one verse.

CLOSER TO YOU

I've become closer to you against
my better judgment, but it was fueled
by my free will.

Haven't met too many that
honor me like you do…
I smile a silly smile when
you enter my mind.

Sometimes I believe you
were sent to me to heal my woes…
But I can't remember what
they are when you draw nearer.

I'm weakened by you
although I'm physically strong.

My knees buckle as I fight
daringly to remain upright…

Then I feel you coming
closer…and closer…
And my breath becomes shortened…

I close my eyes for balance…
When I open them, nothing has changed.

I continue to fight, but
the battle is useless…
All parts of me are not in sync.

My ability to reason has concluded…

My composure is shot !

Then I calm down and
realize that it was meant to be…
Me for you and you for me.

LOVE IS...

Love is…what God gives me everyday.
Not in a special way, or with
words that say…

Love is…not something equally expressed,
I must confess…
It can sometimes cause a mess.

Love is…giving life to a child…
and afterwards, watching
it develop a warm smile.

Love is…giving and never
worrying about taking…
From the bottom of ones
heart without forsaking.

Love is…what we all seek and
hope to one day find.
When I find it, it will truly be mine.

Mine to cherish like nothing
ever seen before…
Something I will give freely
and never ask for more.

Love Lost

Nothing equates to the pain
of losing something you truly love.
Pain greater than 1000 deaths
that reaches down and snatches
your soul from deployable depths.

The nights of sleep lost…
The pounds of muscle reduced
at an incomparable cost…

Never did I ever imagine I
could care so much…
for someone whose touch
melts me after I become flush.

One day I will recover from this funk.
Hopefully, not from a bottle
in a deep drunk…

I feel the mason erecting the
bricks to protect my breast plate.
Will I find love again
before it's too late…

Passion

It's the drive within me
that makes me strong…
The will which makes me
want to go on…

It makes me do things
some can't relate…
Even when my inner
soul is in debate.

It provides me the ability to
love like none before…
Keeps me afloat when my heart is sore.

When I go down hard
and sometimes hit the ground…
It's the thing that lifts me
up to go one more round.

It's those electrifying moments
when our paths do cross…
It provided me the way
when I was so lost.

It's the feeling I got
when our love was new…
It's the feeling that makes
me want to touch you.

It's the thing I would extinguish
my life to give…
Without it, life would be too hard to live.
It's the fire that can't be put out…
It allows my soul to yearn
and not shout !…

It burns in me like an eternal flame…
When times are difficult in
the middle of the game.

It's an indulgence of things
that can not be fulfilled…
It's love; it's anger incurable
by any pill.

Friends and Lovers

We started as neighbors;
proceeded to be friends…
Now we're lovers, what
a Godsend…

Occasionally I laugh when
I think of all the things we've done…
What Joy!…What Fun!…

I flash back and remember
a split second that highlights…
The day I realized we fell in like.

I'd never guessed in a million years…
that I would fall in love with
my closest peer…

A wide spectrum of
foreknowledge came to be…
When I foretold your future with me.

So many years have elapsed…
I yield like an audience
being overwhelmed to clap.

Affinity brought us together
and we mold like provocative clay.

An alliance that we share
that will never give way…

An innocent flirtation
that grew into adulation…
A sensational enchantment
that breeds respectful sentiments…

A staggering Valentine
that blooms anytime…

A phenomenal companion
who's ever so kind…

My days of wistful thinking
are no longer true…
Nostalgic of the day that
you said I do.

My Valentine

No Secret of mine…
Blessed by time.
Known only as my Valentine.

Identified on a special day.
Candy, flowers and cards
in a special way.
Love shared and treasured
truly fine…
Known only as my Valentine.

Grace in pure motion
I once described…
A selection one heart
has that's truly mine.
How can anyone be so kind…
Known only as my Valentine.

A celebration that last
only a day.
My celebration that
lingers—always…
A love and joy that's
forever blind…
Known only as my Valentine.

Seduction

SEDUCTION

Seduction has nothing to do with
the act of sex.
Some that leads many to worry
about the results of tests.

Seduction is a state of being,
not to be confusing with idle
teasing.

Seduction invites sex appeal…
Something that helps broken
hearts heal.

It's a desire not associated
with lust.
It's when two eyes meet and
guarantee trust.

Seduction can be as simple as
holding hands on a first date.
Do it wrong and you might
have to wait.

Seduction can be in the swing
of a woman's hips…
Or watching lipstick applied
to her lips.

Seduction for woman can be
in man's Baritone…
The way he manipulates words
in a song.

But most of all, Seduction for me
might not be the same for you…
It might be something that cradles
your nerve and sinew.

Seduction is like the game of
Cat and Mouse…
One hides, while the other
hunts in the house.

If done correctly,
in a moment's notice…

You'll find love everlasting,
a companion promised.

A KISS

The touch of a feelings glow…
Ask me how I know?

The touch of a feeling glow…
An act that can only be shown.

I gathered myself after
I was sure this person was
the only one to choose…
When we started, I can't remember
whose mouth was whose.

I was lost in the mist…
Never believed anything
so heavenly could come from a kiss.

I look forward to our next
intimate moment again…
Where I won't be able
to tell where her top lip
begins, and where
my bottom lip ends.

Fantasy

I dream with my eyes open,
as you draw near to that place
that is here…

Dominated by everything
but sight and sound…
I've often tried not to awaken
when you come around.

Wherefore are you as I find
myself trapped between
reality and myth.
The only inclination is
knowing that it is you that
I am to be with.

My self prediction or prophecy
as it may…
This dream is so real, I
don't know what to say.

When I think of you my
wishes are unlawful…
I'm reduced to a bootlegger
of love, just short of being pitiful.

My natural rhythm is off as
my mind fluctuates…

I'm at another level,
it's like heaven and
I'm through the gates.

I often dream of you
undeniably so…
Then I find myself getting
into an imminent flow…

I can't take my mind off
what has me frantically…
Going around and around
to the point I cannot see…

I have trespassed and invited
you into my space.
With the time of my existence
I have no seconds to waste…

The disintegration of my
thoughts and wishes will never come…
They keep me alive or otherwise
I would be done.

Making Love

My body speaks to you…

It doesn't matter if you are
black, white, red, yellow or brown.

My body speaks to you…

My language is English and
yours another…

My body speaks to you…

The language our bodies
communicates; the sounds they make…
The aroma they generate…

My body speaks to you…

Tall, wide, short or small…

My body speaks to you…

Our conversations are
sometimes short…
Usually not containing any torts…

Then we pause…
Moments before an exploding cause…

My body kisses you…

Kisses you in so many
different ways…

My body speaks to you…

Never trying to be harsh…
Always beginning kinda soft.

My body speaks to you…

Our words come in and out…
Once in a while bellowing
a shout!!

My body speaks to you…

We talk til we can't
talk no more…
We remain speechless forevermore…

My body becomes you.

Red

Dark Crimson and blood…

My heart and a valentine's love.

A dark flame that's burning hot !!

Touch it…

I dare not!!!

I Knew

I was sentenced to being
displaced before I saw your face.

Walked alone…

No breath, no home…

My left had no right…

My dark had no light…

The stories I told,
if I dare…
Were always of isolation
and despair.

So many come and gone.
So many times I was alarmed…

Thinking some things did
not appear too fair.
Then I saw you and without
thought, I had so much to bare.

Bare my soul…

Bare my wants…

Bare what I know…

Bare my taunts…

Instant gratification in a
seconds notice…
Here I am like a simple novice.

I knew long before
you had a clue…
That in this life I
would end up with you.

Entrapment and the
widow's web…
Were not needed because
you already had me there…

With…

My honor…

My destiny…

I am displaced no more.
A welcomed place
for me to adore.

Adore' in the modest sense.
I prayed for you shortly
after my repent…

You were given to me
to bond like Crazy has
it glue…

Once a simple novice,
from the earliest day
with you…

I knew…

The Encounter

Full of spice
and quite so nice.

Sizzling hot
to think not.

An attractive glare,
no one dare.

Ask her name
Too shy it's a shame.

The smile on her face
Feel the grace.

Who are you?
No longer blue.

Just passing by
Hoping not to die.

We finally talk
during a short walk.

She shares so much
I am in touch.

She grazed my hand
A move unplanned.

We planned a date
Never too late.

We did it again
Now we're best friends.

She became my darling wife
She is my life.

I would do it again
'Til time has no end.

Family

Sis…

Hey Sis…
Remember when we were
kids and I'd rather meet
my maker than apply on
your cheek a kiss.

Hey Sis…
You are everything I've
imagined a woman to be…
No other woman can compare
to you from what I see.

Hey Sis…
You wear motherhood well…
One day I will share with
you the stories to other
woman I tell.

Hey Sis…
You remind me of mom
just a little…
But some of the things you
do are a bit more frugal.

Hey Sis…
You are a spectacular wife…
Your husband told me that you
are the greatest part of his life.

Hey Sis…
Your children say they truly blessed…
You're everything to them yet.

Hey Sis…
As a child you could
never tender my behind…
But when I did mess up,
you knew how to set me straight
with a few tart lines…

Hey Sis…
I've watched you develop
into a lady so fine…
But better yet a lady so kind.

Hey Sis…
The love I have for you
makes me your greatest fan…
A love only a brother can understand.

Uncles
(Dedicated to Norman Lancaster)

I never had too many, but
the few I had were enough.
They were my link to manhood,
which taught me to capture
the essence of being tough.

They were big brothers and
teachers all molded into one…
They could even be a father
figure and treat you like a son.

The uncles I've had
all did their parts…
Like a fine resin, holding
the family together from the start.

Without notice, they
began to fade away…
Then a bright memory comes
and saves the day.

Thoughts of the great times
we spent together…
Family outings, sporting events,
and all kinds of weather.

I can still remember as
a child seeing you from a far…
Making you one of my secret
heroes I thought ascended
from a star.
The relationship we had
was always neat…
Doing some of the things my
dad and I didn't embark upon
really made our times unique.

MOMMA

When I entered the world
she was first person I saw.
Living my life would be according
to her law.

She dressed me, feed me and
nurtured me everyday.
Loving me unconditionally
was her only way.

Agape' is what it is spiritually called.
She was always there to pick
me up after a fall.

Regardless of what I did good
or bad, she was always there…
If it wasn't right, what a piecing stare.

I might not agree with
everything that she does.
But nothing compares to
a mother's love.

One day she will leave me and I
will try not to cry.
Just having her in my life
is a natural high.

When she passes on, how will
I accept the pain.
The legacy she leaves to me
will be worthy of the gain.

I'll one day take a wife or husband
and watch her smile and grin.
Throughout my life, momma
will always be my best friend.

When momma hurts, I hurt ten fold…
She's stronger than most men,
undoubtedly so…

She taught me so many things—
too many to count.
Stacking them up would be a high mount.

She sacrificed so much to ensure
I was happy…
Combed my hair delicately,
although it was nappy.

I'm a better person because
you have shown me the way.
A part of Momma is revealed
through me each and every day.

Brother

Growing up we had some
endless fights…
To this day, I never knew
who was right.

We fought until our
faces were blood red…
It's only by the grace
of God that no one
ended up dead.

As we grew older, we never
tried to compete…
Too proud to let the other
claim victory and give into defeat.

When I look at you,
I see myself…
Staring endlessly until
I have nothing left.

We share the same genetic traits…
Being related was our bonding fate.

We bonded more and more
as time went on…
With the things that drew
us together to look upon…

In our family we always
knew our place…
Little brother…Big brother…
Trying to keep pace.

When our father was
absent, I always knew what to do…
Become the dominant male
and figure out the right
things to show you…

You are everything I
wished I could be…
I see now that the door
is unlocked and you have the key.

Now I look at you as a father,
leader, husband, teacher in regard…
You learned your lessons well
brother, none of them were too hard.

I've watched many try to
break you, but you won't bend.

Never allowing anyone to
take advantage and know
the things that are within…

As we become older,
we become closer in every way.
Kindly speaking the
words love taught us to say.

Looking back at when
we played in the yard...
And dreamed of fancy cars...

Addressed pretty girls
with respect...

You are a really good
friend, brother—my best!!!

Cousins

We look alike; we act alike…
We're closer than anyone
we could ever meet.
As children, we looked forward
to the games we played
on our streets.

Our child-like demeanor never
seems to disappear…
When we are with each other
growing old is never a fear.

I trust you like no one
ever before…
You are the only one that
I will give the key to my store.

We are family and friends
steadfast and jelled to perfection.
Outside of my siblings
you have my undaunting affection.

Never a stranger, markedly on top…

With the key I gave you,
my store is my heart.

Culture

WASHINGTON, DC

The land where Lincoln
lived and died…
A place where assassins dare hide…

No other city is incased in
such specter of marble so white.
No other city has experienced
such a suburban exodus flight.

Many call this unique place home.
The place where the great marches
of the 60's and 90's was cause to atone.

It has danger; it has excitement…
No other place can duplicate
it's delightment.

It's the sun of the inner
Solar System of Nation States…
Its directs soldiers to guard
foreign gates.

Yet, many criticize it as drug infested.
Not only known criminals get arrested.

It is a city where freedom rings.
Where years ago certain people
could not sing…

It's modeled after from place to place.
It once freely exported hate.

It remained neutral between
the North and South,
Just look at the great leaders house.

This city is renown for its similarity
to Chocolate milk.
It's culture is more enriching
than silk.

A place people find exciting…
Somewhere remarkable, and enticing.

Only miles away from the Chesapeake Bay…
Visitors go there everyday…

It was created from old swamp
land down below…
Once going there you'll
see a wonderful show.

It doesn't have skyscrapers
to define its outline.
Its monuments alone are truly fine.

It has its ups and downs,
and downs and ups…
One after another, political hick-ups.

The Bullets became the Wizards

to mask its connotation to crime.
Go-Go music is its reason
for rhyme.

Day after day, this system goes on…
Silence comes at Arlington
to a Bugles horn…

This isn't a city where the
masses attempt to save face.
I've never been in such a better place.

CHICAGO

She's mystifying and grandeur,
Magnanimous in splendor and how…
Gigantic buildings that make you say wow!!

Full of culture; second to none—
an argument for Los Angeles
and New York City ready to come.

It has everything you are looking for…
Good things, bad things, whatever
you have in store.

You will marvel at her beauty and city
line from a distance on any night.
Seeing her from above may
overwhelm you during any flight.

She is one of the greatest places
anyone can frequent…
Take a lot of money;
need it for rent…

Home to the Bulls, Cubs and Sox,
games in which many people flock.

Her Universities are world renown…
Some of her neighborhoods
appear war torn.

A shoppers paradise will before
you eyes unfold.
The things acquired are truly bold.

Just visiting this Grand city…
Is enough to make anyone Giddy.

RELIGION

A child looked over to his
Uncle in Church and said
"Those people got 'ligion…
I hope to be like that one day"…
The uncle said back
"Say your prayers and
believe in God and it
will come your way".

'Ligion will change your
walk, your talk…
Not make you smart,
but relinquish ones
ability to bark at women
passing by…
Instead, Holiness presents
a new High.

A long lasting encounter with
the Father the Son
and the Holy Ghost…
'Ligion will indeed capture
ones ability and aptitude
to be the most…

And live and dance to
a new song.

Bewildered by how
one ever got along…

Without knowing such
a wondrous Lord.
Magnificent in every way
encapsulating and exciting
never to be bored.

With "ligion comes belief
in things that are
omnipresent, but not seen.

'Ligion alone is not enough…
To save ones soul and
become saved is…
By confessing the love
of Jesus so bold.

Our Land

What would we do if this
land were ours…

We often ponder the idea
of a land; a modern land,
that's culturally ours.

What would our ancestors
do if this land was theirs…

Would they reflect and on
Africa and relive their dreams
of being tribal Kings and Queens.

Would we prosper in this land
of great lands, knowing that we have
never seen the greatest of all lands…

What would we do if this
land were ours…

This land others fail to
understand we help make…
This land we participated with
the original owner's enemies
to annihilate…

What if this land were ours…

Would we develop it
as we want…
Build it strong with
wars that haunt…

If this land were ours, we
would be mystified…
And show we could not
be more gratified.

But this land is ours
and everyone else's to share…
Try to take it away from
me if you dare.

My Flava Ain't Your Flava

I like up and you like down.

I like small and you like big.

I like movies; you like song.
I say short; you say long.

I like dresses; you like pants.

I like hair; you like bald.

I like dark; you prefer light.
I prefer the ground; you prefer heights.

You like it hot; I want it cold.

You like it spicy; I like it mild.
You prefer adult-like; I harbor
my inner child…

You are always calm;
sometimes I like to play…
You want it at night; I prefer the day.

You like the front; I like the rear.
You call me honey; I call you dear…

You love cake; I love pie.
You want everlasting life;
I'm not afraid to die.

You like TV; I prefer books.
One day you smiled and I was totally hooked.

We are different as night and day…
My Flava ain't your Flava…
It's not too bad that things are that way.

NOTES

So many want justice...
What will be the driving
force to protect us from us.

Once upon a time we feared
the Klan...
Once upon a time the Klan
sparked fear into our hearts
in this land.

Castration, mutilation, humiliation...
In this place we call our nation...

I have no fear of the Klan in
this day and time.
My only fear is of those
whose image is like mine.

Black men continue to kill
more of their own.
Place like DC, New York, La,
and the other places we call home.

The groups we once feared
are now obsolete...
Regardless of the numbers
of committees or how they meet.

The old talk of race
and war still barks on…
Like an old Junk yard dog…

Too old…
Too wary to chase anyone…

Yet the war rages on and
is fueled from within…
Black men killing Black men…
What a pity, what a sin.

Some blame hopelessness;
some blame despair.
Innocent people dying; robbed
of their lives—this isn't too fair.

We once asked why is this so…
Then we conceded and accepted
this as the status quo.

Who's the real guilty
party in all of this?
We're all guilty because we
sit back and pretend this doesn't exist.

For years I've kept score
even when I thought there
was no hope…
How can we not keep things
like this in our mental notes.

GETTING IT ON…

One day I got my groove on
Just before I got my dance on
and my eat on…

Or was it when I got my sleep on
After getting my drink on
in preparation of getting my party on…

While there, I had such a
great time that I got my
laugh on…

Then later, I got my Mack on
How many more ways can I
get it on…
I have no idea until I am forewarned

But as a child in school
I got my study on…
Then I got my football and track on,
and after twelve years,
I got my graduation on…

But then, I moved on and got
my college on…
Then, my interview on…
Which helped me get my job on…

Now I got my wife on…
Right after I got my marriage on…

Good thing all of that came before
I got my children on…

One day, I'll get my house on
and live a long prosperous life
that will lead to me getting
my retirement on…

Then I'll get my travel on…
and grow old until the
day I pass on.

JAZZ

Do Whop…Be Whop…Do be do…
Were the words the musician sang,
As he played a mindful song
with his talented gang.

What kind of music I'm I hearing…
My ears, my feet are peering.

It has a beat unlike rock and pop…
It will make you tap your feet
right out of your sox.

Those who craft this stuff, do it
because it means so much…
The more I listen, the less I understand
Maybe it waz part of
the grand ole plan.

Grand ole plan you might ask…
An introduction to a form of
communication that will last.

An expression of the way
some live in peace.
An uncomplicated way to please
in comfort with no tranquility cease.

Listen closely, and you will hear…
Different sounds that will move
you and make cloudy things clear.

How did it get its name anyway?
Was it from listening to the slaves
back in the day.

It is the only true form
of American music culture.
Just as natural as things
produced by nature to heighten us…

THE HOOD

From whence we came,
So many look for blame.
With exception to those who
live there…
Once entering there is
no reason to stare.

In foreign countries
they call them ruins,
Many want to live there,
but can not get a shoe in…

In America they are called ghettos…
Now these places are becoming
land to be sold, for
the erection of Condos.

Growing up, children never
knew they were societies last…
They could not define
societal class.

From the outside looking
in, it appears that structures
will never be stood.
In modern times, kids
call these places—The Hood.

Old verses new; new verses old…
Look at the things being sold.

People born, people dying…
So many stories told, wonder
whose lying.

The truth comes from within,
Just ask any kin…
Survival of the fittest
is the way of life.
When you read the paper,
don't believe the Hype.

Drugs pour in million of dollars,
Ever heard a crack baby holler…

Everyone exploits the revenue
that can be gathered,
The suburbs are the answer
to thwart family shatter.

Twenty is the mythical age
for men's expiration…
Will Twenty-one bring jubilation.

The powers to be have
abandoned them all.
They sit in the Congressional
wings awaiting their fall.

In this place where great
men once stood...
A place young people call
—The Hood.

Black

Two of the most wondrously
beautiful things in the universe
are a Black Stallion and a Black Pearl.
The Moors were black, and they
almost ruled the world.

Think if you will, the undaunting
strength of a Black hole, or that
luscious thing called oil–Black Gold.

The word Black is rarely used
to describe things that are good.
Mostly it's used in a negative
context—causing many to
be misunderstood.

The best way to describe Black
is to describe something
literally dark…
Like the color of a Walnut tree's bark.

But Black is often described as
something bad…
Identified with people
who are always had…

Black is viewed as sooty, dirty,
depressing and somber…

Myths alone that make it hard
to find a good neighbor.

Black is seen as wicked, sullen
atrocious and horrible.
Not everything associated with
Black is deployable.

Black is synonymous with
fiendish, inhuman and devilish…
It's no wonder many Black
people are afraid to wish…

Black has a direct connotation
to being sinful, diabolic and amoral…
But then again, that depends
whose definition is being used
to prompt and create upheaval…

Black is also seen as monstrous,
nefarious and hopeless…
Is this a color being defined
or just pure rhetoric.

Black is a color, nothing
more, nothing less…
It's not something that
should be used to create
obligalatory comments.

Diamonds are formed from
the Blackest of all coal…
Being a diamond in the rough
is my lifetime goal.

Tranquility

Shadow

It follows me like a new puppy.

I lose it amongst the dark corners,
but it appears without warning.

My image in every way…
It follows me around
from day to day.

Every once in a while
I forget it's there…
Every once in a while
it causes me to stare…

Is that really me?
I often ask myself…
If it could speak would
it reveal my inner self?…

This dark friend we all have…
Watching us endlessly
to unreachable depths.

When it goes away we
look for it to again appear…
If it doesn't, something bad
is lurking near.

It's our silent friend, the only
one thing we can truly trust.
It will never give you an
opinion or ever make a fuss…

My image appearing from
a strange angle for me…
Looking away; not minding my deeds.

Then I realize, this ghostly character
has only one thing it could be…
An angel sent from above
to watch over me.

Running

An infinite stride that
frees me from the world…

Solitude becomes my passion.

My heart races, then
calms to a steady beat.

My lungs adjust and regulate
my performance to a measure
of consistency know only
by runners who meet.

I become one with the wind…
It circles me…
Pushing me forward and challenging
me to resist all the while…

I dare myself to quit knowing
that I would have not gained a thing.

No pain to feel…
Just my youth being stretched…

Then I stop and awaken
to a new day…
Tomorrow's venture is
hardly a step away.

SALVATION

Salvation is free…
Just ask for it and you will see.

Salvation is free…
Being generous is what
I've always wanted to be.

Salvation is free…
Get on your knees and pray with me.

Salvation is free…
Ask the lord and he will
provide your needs.

Salvation is free…
The virtuous woman and
Godly man have a blessed seed.

Salvation is free…
No matter how many things
you've done called good deeds.

Salvation is free…
The best gift ever bestowed upon me.

Sensation

A collage of all
anyone could wish…

Fondness and passion…
The tenderness of a soft kiss…

A lad and damsel whose
affection has no fee.

Floating infinitely like a raft
on a calm sea.

Joy

Everything that embodies jubilance
comes from joy.

A wedding day…

The birth of a child…

A new job…

A high grade on a test…

Joy in its magnificence alone
is thrilling.
Looking for it and finding it
is modestly fulfilling.

Joy brings laughter…

Joy brings smiles…

Joy is finding God…

Joy is finding a child that's lost…

Joy is feeling well after
being sick.
Joy is rooting fro a team
that's not getting licked.

Joy is Ice Cream and cake…
Joy is ice skating on a lake.

Joy is meeting a clown at the circus…

Or even more, Joy is
buying candy from the store.

Joy is all the things from above.

Joy can be found with
someone's love.

Complexity

Gilded Horse
(O.J. Simpson, Mike Tyson, Michael Jackson, Clarence Thomas)

The gilded horse has
four twisted legs…

One broken…

One amputated…

One Crooked…

One bowed…

In the 90's this
horse lost face…
It was too humiliated
to race.

It raced against another
thoroughbred and broke a leg…
Fortunate for him
he did not end up dead.

It ran through airports
as a young stallion would…

Rented cars…
Befriended movie stars.

Until its life raged
a war of violence…
And a mare and young stud
were lost in the balance.
He one day tripped others
and was disqualified…
It maintained its innocence
although some thought he'd lied.

This horse was jaded
until one day until one day
his leg was amputated.

As a young pony
this horse was competitive
beyond belief…
No other pony was
ever held in such high esteem.

In the days of its
Derby's best…
It lost status for touching
a young pony where he rest.

The next race was slightly booked.
Then the owner noticed
his leg was crooked.

At the premiere stages of
this horse's performance
he could trot, and race
with them all…

No contest would be
the judges call.

Until one day he
teased a mare in tow…
When the gates opened
the orchestrators noticed
his leg was bowed.

An awry horse
he soon became…
Gilded and branded and
placed in the stable of shame.

JUSTICE

There once was a lady I
learned so much about…
She was groomed to protect me,
ensuring my rights were
never cast out.

She was blinded to enforce
the laws of the day.
Not being able to see—making
it her quest that things
were judged the right way.

Rich man, poor man, she
really didn't care…
When they all stood before her
there was suppose to be nothing to fear.

Was there ever true balance
in the world we live in…
Visit any court day to day
and witness the hearing therein.

As a child I was falsely accused;
went to jail and then to court,
just a tad confused.

I knew justice would protect me
so I waited for my case to unfold…

I knew about this lady,
so I believed what I was told.

Probation! after hearing the gavel slam.
Probation for what?
How did I get into this jam.

Then as an adult, I was arrested again
while walking through my
neighborhood too bold...
This time when I went to court,
I saw justice peep from
behind her blindfold.

At that instance what
was I to think?

I swallowed like hell, but could
not get the lump in my throat to sink.

From this point, justice was
becoming an euphemism for
putting us in jail.
Every-time I heard the
word it became came synonymous
with hell.

For those who do not understand
what I'm trying to say...
I challenge you to visit a
courtroom on any given day.

Keeping Score

Regardless what happens as the
days go by, the score continues to
be 400+ to none.

Some contributions are hidden
like a shadow in the shade,
endlessly looking at those
accomplishments evade…

The score is 400+ to none.

When grace is won,
the score changes to 400+ to 1.

Momentarily it appears good
things are due; another accomplishment
makes it 400+ to 2.

An accusation or law violation is
alleged; with nothing more to pledge…

The score card is deducted by
more than one.
The sum is once again 400+ to none.

A more modern day is here.
The score will never be closed
by what is brought to bare.

In difference to what I've
heard from some, the score
will always appear to be 400+ to none.

They Were Chosen

Several men got off a
train one dark night in Tuskegee…
Some of the greatest minds known…

A project presumed to fail…
Hearts determined to exceed…

Achieving what no other
before them had, and will
ever do again…

They were the chosen…

Several kids entered a school
in Arkansas on a bright day
as the world watched…

Their will was unmatched
by any that resembled them…

Hard on the surface;
gentle from within…
Hurdled many who
openly exploited sin.

They were the chosen.

Not yet adult, far
from being kids…

Amidst the anguish
of a brutal state which
proudly exported racial hate…

Someone special entered the
plateau of higher learning
in Mississippi under the guard
of the Constitutional police…

None failed; all exceeded…

They were the chosen.

He dreamed the impossible dream…
He spoke a language of unity…

A leader of uncompromised
integrity and focus…

A prodigy at any level.

A man who feared God…

A king who gave his
life for the fight of equality.

He was chosen.

She led many to freedom
in a way Amtrak never could.

Had faith to do the
things no one would…

A conductor before Porters
became common place…
Her train was always on schedule
with no lives to waste…

She was chosen…

Some of them died…
They once all cried.

They fought battles that
would bring an Army to brink…
Years later many would come to think…

These people were more
than special because what they gave…

Freedom!…

Liberty!…

And happiness all the same…

They were chosen.

They were scholars, soldiers
athletes, statesmen, and entertainers
who dealt with the most
compelling issue of modern time–race.

They might not have been
the most eloquent or best
at their craft…
Yet they had the fortitude
markedly superior to those
who said they were inferior
and would not last…

They were chosen…

Chosen to magnify a
people's quest to be known.
If not for the chosen ones,
our futures would not have a home.

Things People See

The eyes are the gateway of the soul.
Only if the eyes could speak,
what stories would be told.

Seeing ladies on the street corner…
Watching men buy happiness
for the meaning of a dollar.

Watching older men cheat with
younger women that they meet.

Trying to hide the way people lie…
Peering deeply at the way some
people die.

Seeing unjustly things unfold…
Theft from someone's billfold.

Seeing awful crimes committed…
Giving witness to those befitted.

Watching children go without…
Seeing some hungry as their
stomachs pout.

Seeing joy on a wedding day…
Experiencing happiness on a
child's birthday.

Watching some fade away in shame…
Seeing illegal transactions during
a political campaign.
Seeing the sun set and moon rise…
Watching waves come in
during a high tide.

Seeing fire destroy a families dream…
Seeing the expression of a frightened
woman's scream.

Seeing two lovers hug and kiss…
Seeing the things around them
that they will miss.

Watching grown men play golf…
Seeing an airplane take-off.

Watching animals run through
the woods…
Seeing the things that are misunderstood.

Watching a sporting event with glee…
The wonders of the things people see.

Youth Gone Mad

What's going on with today's youth.
Things are happening so suddenly
all this rage and spoof...

Being teased by the people they meet.
Later conflict that encourages packing heat.

Once the damage is done.
Many parents blame music, movies,
computer games for concealing a gun.

People die and there is no remorse...
The some it up like these kids
had no choice.

When gang banging seemed
the norm in the hood.
Suburbanites thought the people
were misdirected and not misunderstood.

Oh, the things they were
labeled and called.
No one wanted to address the
problems as lives began to fall.

Then the violence changed
locations and moved where it never lived.
America wake up! and began to give...

Give in to excuses of why
youngsters chose to kill.
It was easier to kill others
than extinguish oneself with pills.

Have the youth really gone mad…
The answer is unclear; some of
the good children have turned bad.

The nation is being introduced to
places never thought existed before…
The focus is now the small town
instead of the big city floor.

Discipline remains absent
and parents wonder why…
If the problem isn't soon resolved
we will here a nation cry.

Someone must account for the
things that are going wrong.
The next incident is cooking and
awaiting to sound its gong.

Parents are afraid to tender
a young child's tail.
Fear of charges of abuse
and a trip to jail…

What's going on with the
youth of today…

Totally lost and using
violence as their way.

What's going on with parents
is the answer…
Save the children and cure the cancer.

AFFIRMATIVE ACTION

So many were angry when a
terrible deed was corrected.
Isn't that why we went
to the polls to get certain
politicians elected?

Balance in civilization has its place.
Something that should be not
be defined by race.

To affirm is to ensure justice
and make better.
You would never know this by
the editorials and all the letters.

Doing the right thing made so
many people angry.
Reversing the right thing
was a mockery that many
could not see.

My…My…My…does anyone
know the reason why,
It appeared so hard to try…

It was designed to protect certain
people from being held back.

Education was not what
they lacked.

As the scales moved
towards balance…
Certain people were disturbed
and tried to eradicate things with malice.

Rage sing throughout
the corporate halls…
It became the catalyst to
change the laws.

Things are not as they once were…
Let's turn the clock back to
the 1960's and not thereafter.

I'm sure this would please many.
Except those who want to
live in harmony.

Neither side will gain or lose…
Be careful which side you choose.

Freedom

A statue holding a torch
that exemplifies…
A new found life that
no one will defy.

13 stripes and 50 stars…
democracy fought for with
so many scars.

The mad rush from all
corners of the globe…
Behold…
A search for something no
one could feel or hold.

Some never know what it
means because it was
never compromised…
A word to the wise…

It can be taken away
with the flicker of a flash.
Then watch it removed
and reduced to ash.

Several men endorsed a
document that told…

A story all men could not relate
to from being sold.

Not merchandise or anything nice.
Just a life that never quite lived
up to what should have been their slice…

No not pie…
Freedom is worth several lives
so no one should die.

It's disheartening to be free
with ones mind in a jail.
Thinking you're free, but
actually living in a hell.

Being free is symbolic of being
spirited and exploring new heights…
No shackles, no bars…
No left, no right.

Maybe the only freedom
anyone has is in the guff…
Until our souls are sent to earth
until our bodies have had enough.

The land of plenty…
A bounty for all who call.
Yet some are caged to become
beggars on the streets and even
the Capitol Mall…

Freedom can be a bad thing when
the prisons of the mind and
institutions set us free…
No reform, character lost is what
I have come to be…

However the greatest gift anyone
was given was the freedom of choice.
The ability to make the right decisions;
to express with a loud voice.

A voice that resounds so loud…
That you become weightless while
floating amongst the clouds.

What If?

What if I could give you
everything that's mine…
Even find a way to give
you borrowed time.

What if there was no
prejudice and all people
were considered equal…
Would we live in a
wonderful place absent of evil.

What if you were me
and I were you…
Would we be the same
as we imagine ourselves
from our point of view…

What if it was impossible
for someone to make you mad…
Would it be normal to
be forever happy and never sad…

What if we only measured
the beauty one possessed from within…
And all things otherwise
would be a sin…

What if you could be
perpetually protected from harm…
Would your life be a
prison or like a charm…

What if there was no love
and we could only express like…
Would we care more
regardless of who was our type…

What if everything were a treasure
with nothing to forsake…
Imagine if we never knew
the sentiment called hate…

What if we were not too prideful
and proud to expose who we are…
Would we all be too sensitive
and instead of close more far…

What if we live forever
until time stood still…

What if there was no hunger
and food were available
for the many…
Would we waste it when
it appears we have plenty…

If is the smallest big
word ever made…
Imagine if we lived our

conscious how many lives
we would save…

When we use words that
are contemplative and verbose,
chose another word instead
of if like suppose.

Women

She

She entered my life one day…
I was breathless with nothing to say.

She walked out of my dreams
descriptive of my prayers…
Seeing her for the first time
caused me to stare.

She was faith, hope, joy and
happiness all rolled into one.
When darkness fell she
became the sun.

Oh, how she exuberates
my soul…
If it's love, she really
has a hold…
of everything that comprises
what I am.
If she ever lets go, the
fall would be a slam.

She entices me like nothing
ever felt before.
My Cherie Amour…
I adore…

The love she exudes
makes me high.
I'm on cloud nine and
I never learned how to fly.

What she does to me is
too hard to explain.
The wild beast in me
has finally been tamed.

She's truly Angelic
from where I sit…

I must admit…

She's the missing piece
that makes me whole–
A perfect fit.

Words like beautiful,
gorgeous and pretty
are too small.
What she is cannot
be called…

She reminds me of a rose,
Nature's most perfect flower…
Or the first thing that
comes to mind seeing a
rainbow after an afternoon shower.

Women

If I live one thousand life-times,
that still would not be enough
to fully marvel your kind.

I've envisioned you tall and small…

And walking from side to side…
My eyes and mouth can't decide–
whether to look or talk
or talk or look…

Every time I see you, I
immeasurably hooked.

When you speak…
I often buckle from being weak.
Never able to explain why
you're so unique…

When you smile…
I instantly become a child…
Awaiting your cradle and caress.

What man would expect less…

When you accept me as
Your mate.

I'll never forget the date
And introduce you to my beloved way.

I'm yours on any day.

The pleasures I'll give you'll
Never have to be sold…
When I think of what I'll
give you, I don't know whether
to implode or explode.

Remembrance of when I saw
you first…
Feeling like I was
going to burst…

Oh me…Oh me…Oh my!…

I don't know whether to smile or cry.

Only when I become suspended
in time, will I be undoubtedly
quenched by your kind.

HER

It was like watching a tennis
game go back and forth as
my neck sprung repeatedly.
My eyes went right to left
unimpededly.

Or was it like watching the
waves come in and go out
on a sleek beach.
Her moves where sweeter than
anything I would come to meet.

Oooh…ooow…were the thoughts
created by my mind's fling.
It must be a man thing…

Maybe one day I will
take a poll.
A continual intake of this kind
of thing has to take its toll.

Look, but don't touch…
the sensitivity factor is way up…
She walks by…
Was that a spark in her eye…

I'll open any door to let her in,
My thoughts alone just might be a sin.

The sweet nectar of her scent
drunkens me overwhelmingly,
But from the annals of my darkest
wants, I must act politely.

I see her equal every quarter
of a decade.
My feelings and thoughts
are the same–mind already made.

A walk, a sway, a turn, a gesture…
A whisper, a pucker, a smile; her laughter.
A song, a picture, a description, whatever
may appear stronger.
When she leaves my view,
I pray her visit will last longer.

Sometimes satisfaction comes in
the microcosmic of time spent…
That gives me sweet dreams
that consume my lonely moments.

She was like pure music played
so beautifully.
Each note struck with grace
crafted so eloquently.

A song that lures all men to sing…
Lyrics that confess how they
would love to be her King.

Lady

I got butterflies as she
approached me...
My eyes could not interpret
what my mind wanted me to see.

She was definitely part
of the plan God made
to smile on man...

The lady of the day had appeared.
I dropped to my knees
and gave thanks she was here...

She was once a woman...
Now a lady at last.
The more I think of her,
the more my heart beats fast.

A radiant light from
this lady gleams...
I must tell myself, things
are not what they seem...

Then I paused and thought
whether anything created could
ever produce something better.
But I'm happy all the same,
down to the letter...

Meeting and seeing her
was a true joy.
When we got close, she
made me her toy.

The perfect gentleman I became.
The perfect gentlewoman she
was–seeking no fame.

The statuesque model for all
young girls to emulate.
An urge to be a lady that just
can't wait.

Glamorous, persistent and filled
with glee…
The only one who can
fulfill my needs.

I've waited countless days,
hours and moments for her to arrive.
Sometimes the periods were
so long, I thought I would die.

I'm calmer now that she has
appeared and cured me of my ordeal…
I'm so excited that this instant
has become surreal.

The lady of my life…
Everything I wanted and more.
The composite being that arrived
at my door.

BEAUTY

I replay your smile
over and over again…
A treasure that sets
my soul a blaze…

I replay every curve of
your silhouette's symmetry.
Nothing ever seen before
can match the aura
of it all…

I feel your lips against mine
moments after our kiss has ended.
Although our mouth's
have yet to meet.

The thought rules me
like a forgotten peasant
being overcome by the majesty
of the Queen of Queens.

A school boy's sparkle
that's rare, and not often seen…

The scent of you
spins me like a desert wind.

I will take you to the
depths of the unknown…

Nothing more could
I ever endure…

I'm confused between wrong
and right and right and wrong…
The words of your mouth
are indeed my song.
You are mine to treat with
tenderness and hold dear…

The things dreams make clear.

BLACK WOMAN

You are a full moon
in a desert night,
You are an effervescent
Sun to warm a Spring day.

I've heard you called
Ebony and Mahogany,
but those words were never
befitting to me.

You're God's greatest work
of art.
Set apart, a glow and
vision that makes men hark.

The very thought of you
caresses my heart and soul
to inaccessible levels.

How could anything be so
precious, yet so bold.
Worth more than platinum, never
mistaken for gold.

The Ancient world made
you her Queen.
Not withstanding the things
today that are seen.

Look at the inner strength
you've mustered.
More than enough
to make Samson flustered.

From the Nile to the Niger,
From the Atlanta to
the Pacific and places in
between…
The creator knew what he
was doing when he made
you so keen.

One could think for centuries
to conger all the ways to
describe your magnificence.
But for the most men,
it really doesn't make a difference.

Viewing your image
is grace in motion.
I've loved you forever…
the after thought
is my potion.

THE DRESS

For the first time ever,
my mind drew a blank.
I never saw it coming; I was
unprepared, I was flanked.

It came slowly out of the shade
the Sun provided several trees.
A calm wind blew gently, as
it parted a few leaves.

Then it stood still, motionless,
watching me guess.
Tempting me to move–wondering
if I had anything left.

Its silhouette was a new
vision for me.
Prompting a smile…
Causing me to grin with glee.

At a moments glance, I would
have testified that you were
Leonardo's masterpiece…
Ready for my heart and
soul to feast.

Yet leaving me vulnerable
and infant-like…
How could I not be your type.

Then you moved towards
me and I started to shimmer.
Hopelessly praying that your
actions would bring you nearer.

I cannot say that I am
indiscriminately attracted to you.
If I had wings, you would be
the over-flights I flew.

I'm too afraid to be embarrassed,
and I can feel my mouth getting dry.
You're more beautiful than
the wonders of the sky.

I often riddle, who else
could this be for…
Then I confess, I am the benefactor.

Sometimes the things I
think can animate my scene.
When I anticipate you coming
to me in that dress so green.

Beautiful

Many terms and sayings have
been used to identify those
things that spark us beyond belief.

We often compose our overwhelming
thoughts and gestures to the
finest work of nature at its best…
Like what we are doing
is a test unlike the rest.

If I could reach down into
the deepest places never
discovered by our own kind…
What significance would
any of this have in time.

It's a cloud, a bird, a flower
or view…
Since the beginning I've
been in total awe of you.

What I see renders me
without words!…

I can't express
through my actions
the new feelings I have…

You bring me joy
When I'm sad.

Once again, I search trying
to find the right expression
to describe something new…
A different way to paint you…

In my mind…

In my heart…

In my soul…

But nothing I can think
of will do…

True elegance beyond words
is what I realized I see.
It's not up to me…

You were made the
way you are to enlighten
that special one…

The significant other
to honor the blessing adorned
on you by the creator of all.
Once again, it's not my call…

To say that you're something
like never before…

Hopefully those that
are jealous will not deplore.

What you are and will
always be…
Truly too lovely to
put into words by me.

PRETTY AND NICE

I chose pretty over nice,
pretty caused me to look at her twice.

Nice didn't care how I looked…
Pretty went fishing and
I was hooked.

Nice never commanded much respect.
Pretty had me with a different affect.

Nice promised to take care
of me all the life long.
Pretty reminded me of a bird's song.

Nice would ensure my house was
a home.
Pretty caused me to be alone.

Nice put God first
and me second…
Pretty was never taught
that lesson.

Nice enveloped me like
an Army in pursuit…
Pretty was not concerned about
that sort of thing, to her the
point was moot.

Nice wanted to show the
mother she could be…
Pretty was more focused on
her figure for all to see.

Pretty was the joy of every man,
an outer appearance that attracted
many fans.

Nice never had anyone look twice;
once you got to know her, she
was full of spice.

Nice lived a peaceful and
eventful life.
Pretty never experienced happiness
or true love, just a life of strife.

Oneness

My Wife

You are…

Flesh of my flesh.
The beat of my heart.
The center of my soul.
The essence of my joy…

A part of me just as Eve
was a part of Adam.
A oneness shined on
and blessed by the creator.

The love of loves…
My Queen and very
best friend…

My eternity and infinity…

Marriage Pledge

All that I am I give to you…

All that I have I share with you…

You are a part of me
created from my flesh and bone.

I will treasure our union
until time has no end.

My eyes have trapped
the true vision of you that
is the envy of all men.

The world will know that
we are one…

I stand here today to confess
and embrace this moment that
we share with our clan.

My love will never be in doubt…

My best friend is you–
My life long partner.

I will cherish the simple
things and think out those that
are compelling during ardent times…

Today I pledge my love and
myself to you until the end…
I pray I live one hundred years
and you live one hundred years plus one…
So I will never endure the vicious
pain that will come from not having
you near…
With you I have no fears.

I am one with you my special dear…

The One

A dazzle, flash, flicker and glare…

A sparkle, glow, scintillate and gleam…
More than it would ever seem.

A bawl, bellow, chant and cheer…

The clamour, roar, scream and yell…

I began to hum and trill…
My darling made me thrill.

I was frozen abide and had
to stand fast.
The glance of an eye was all
it took to cast.

I attempted to move, but
my actions were to cease.
Suddenly I felt my endurance increase.

Grasp, grab, kidnap
me and seize…
Can't remember being so pleased.

A touch that feels relaxing
never to compensate.
A frolic that hardly arrived too late.

To adore, appreciate, cherish
and hold dear…
A treasure too valuable not to care.

A donation of gratitude
to mend a wail…
An introduction to love
that only hails…

An adoption to convey
anyone's deepest sins…
I'm so elated, where do I begin.

The youthful person
that replaced the old me.
From the start I've jumped with glee.

An ornamental, elegant and
exquisite brimful thief…
Who pilfered my heart
the second we meet.

Becoming A Man

I learned to swim by being thrown
in the deep end.
Knowing that if I did not
get it right, I would be thrown
back in again.

I learned to ride a bike by
being pushed down a hill…
It was my first time–absent
were the training wheels.

I learned about sex from
the things I see…
Watching examples from day to
day on T.V.

I learned to drive on the Express-way
in an old car…
It was a good thing for all
that I wasn't going too far.

I learned that humility was a
thing that wouldn't last…
Just like all the men in my
family from the past.

I learned that not all people
are truly my friend…

Not even some that I
will call my kin.

I learned that love is something
too hard to explain.

I learned if it's not given
life has nothing to gain.

I learned to work hard
and give my best.
I learned to stay away from
clique's and being like the rest.

I learned to raise my children–a
job that must be done well.
I learned that love and discipline
will keep them out of jail.

I learned to be free and
not build a wall.
I learned to pick myself
up after a fall.

I learned that a good education
is truly a must…
I learned that without it,
my dreams would be a bust.

I learned that my word is
the most precious thing I can give…

I learned that integrity defines
my character–not telling a fib.

I learned that I must challenge
things that are not right.
I learned that I can win without a fight.

I learned most of all that I must
be all that I can…
I learned that I grew up to be
an understanding man.

Nature

Nature

She nourishes all things with
what she shares…
Too much to anticipate
with an overwhelming flare…

She's the earth; the cosmos,
a mother to all…
She's the main reason trees stand tall.

She's a macrocosm of motherhood
like nothing before…
She's a megacosm of universal
things viewed from our shores.

There's nothing she doesn't occupy.
She's even right there with
you the day you die…

She's mysterious, alchemistic,
enigmatic and puzzling…
Stand back and view all
the things that are so dazzling.

We gravitate to what
she provides in mass…
Then remain speechless and
moved to the point of flabbergast.

When we are down she
provides the ambulatory
care to make us better…
During any season, we'll
forget what's the matter…

She has no peer competitor
that we will ever meet…
This charismatic lady who
is truly beatific and sleek…

A ROSE

Her pedals are the sweet
kisses of Nature at her best…
A Rose can never be confused with
any other flower–she flourishes
as a stand-alone, an entity of her own.

She is a relic of yesterday…
A gift for today…
And a blessing for tomorrow…

She defines love in its purest form.
She represents serenity
to a broken heart.
She brings joy when we
expect not.

A Rose, nothing else provides a
scent that enlightens the shrewdest
of beings…

Replaces frowns with smiles,
and unpleasantries with joy…

A Rose can beautify the darkest
of Black Holes,
and become enchanting to
the fairest of the fairest.

Yet, strong enough to withstand
any adversity other than pain…
She heals pain, with nothing to gain.

A Rose, what a generous
present from above…
Something special–one of
the lords most wondrous hugs.

WINTER

He is the mightiest of his kind…
transcends everything known in time.

He's arrogant, bold, harsh,
intimidating and fearless.
He'll freeze your butt off
and render you speechless.

Fall is his embryo and Spring
his morning after…
He put Summer to sleep for a
few hundred years–what a disaster.

He will entice you with a make
believe Summer or Spring day…
Sometimes remnants of Fall
may get in his way.

People protect themselves from him…
Animals go to sleep to avoid him…
We add layers that rob us of being slim.

He frequently strands us from
station to station…
Yet our greatest celebration
evolves with his creations…

Snowflakes…Ice skating…
White covered trees
To name three…

He shortens our days
and lengthens our nights…
Huddles us around the fireplace
in warmth without fright.

He's an old man who seems ageless…
If it were not for Spring, his
beauty would be peerless.

He's hard not to adore…
His mystery has led
many to explore…

The outer limits of his seasonal bliss…
Anticipate his winds…
They can be a tantalizing kiss.

FALL

What is it about this season
that makes us so grim…
Is it because Summer seemed
to disappear without a whim.

The nights become crisp and
days of warmth grow slighter.
Nature brings death to many
things–none dare to fight her.

Baseball comes to an
end and Football starts…
Which one is truly America's
past-time in everyone's heart.

The beauty of Autumn leaves
with foliage changes…
Rain becomes snow in
Winter-like exchanges.

She is often not given credit
for what she gives the world…
This season called Fall
provides an alluring twirl.

She holds her own amongst
Summer, Winter and Spring.

Hey, without her,
Winter could not sing.

She is not given glory
like those before her…
But she provides precious
moments that sometimes
causes people to stir…

Stir in memories everlasting
of high school and college
outings that are forever wanting.
Time gone by that was
indeed very promising.

SEEDLINGS

Scattered from here to eternity…
Laying dormant in the mist
of soil and stone…

An Angel squeezed a cloud and
caused it to rain.
The rain nourished the
seedlings and they reached
upward and rejoiced…
And gave thanks to God.

Thankful that they will
be fruitful and multiply
and provide an abundant
offering to mankind.

Spring

She rids away Winter's great chill,
the time of year that brings such a thrill.

She represents the birth of a new day…
Nature's coming out party, to say
good things are on the way.

She melts snow to become food
for the rose…
Invites us to feel new grass
under our toes.

Gives birds new songs to sing…
their voices in our ears do ring.

Her breath is sweet and
makes everyone smile…
At her best, out of us,
she can bring the child.

No matter where you are
she touches you the same way.
She represents the birth of a new day.

SUMMER

She can synch anything
she touches,
And in a flicker bring people
out into the wilderness in bunches.

She will remind you of Spring,
and make you think of Winter
as some awful thing.

She will draw you to the beach,
and having you yearning
for a Georgia peach.

She can be joy and agony
all in one,
But when she's gone you'll
miss her bright sun.

www.ingramcontent.com/pod-product-compliance
Lightning Source LLC
LaVergne TN
LVHW041707060526
838201LV00043B/612